MACHINES ON THE MOVE

DIGGERS

by Jenna Lee Gleisner

TABLE OF CONTENTS

Words to Know 2

Digger 3

Let's Review! 16

Index 16

I0805999

tadpole books

WORDS TO KNOW

arm

bucket

digs

dumps

lifts

rolls

DIGGER

A digger is big.

track

It rolls.

The arm goes out.

bucket

The bucket has teeth.

It digs.

It lifts.

It dumps.

LET'S REVIEW!

Diggers are big machines! What is this digger doing?

INDEX

arm 7
bucket 9
digs 11
dumps 15
lifts 13
rolls 5